Never Rub Noses With a Narwhal

An Alliterative Arctic ABC Book

Ruth Wellborn

Illustrated by

Morgan Wellborn

Best Regards
Ruth Wellborn

This book is dedicated to Freya and Juno, Iver, Kailash, and Corbin. And to Wes and Colleen thank you for the love, support and encouragement, and most especially to Morgan for sharing his incredible artistic talent in this book.

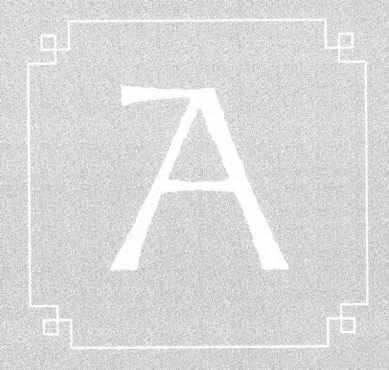

AN AIRPLANE ARRIVES
AT AKLAVIK AIRPORT.

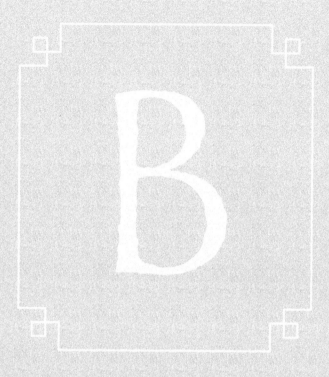

BLUBBER HELPS BELUGAS
STAY BUOYANT IN THE
BEAUFORT SEA.

A CARIBOU CALF CAPERS
THROUGH CLUSTERS
OF CLOUDBERRIES.

DUCKS DEFTLY
DIVERT AROUND A
DIAMOND MINE.

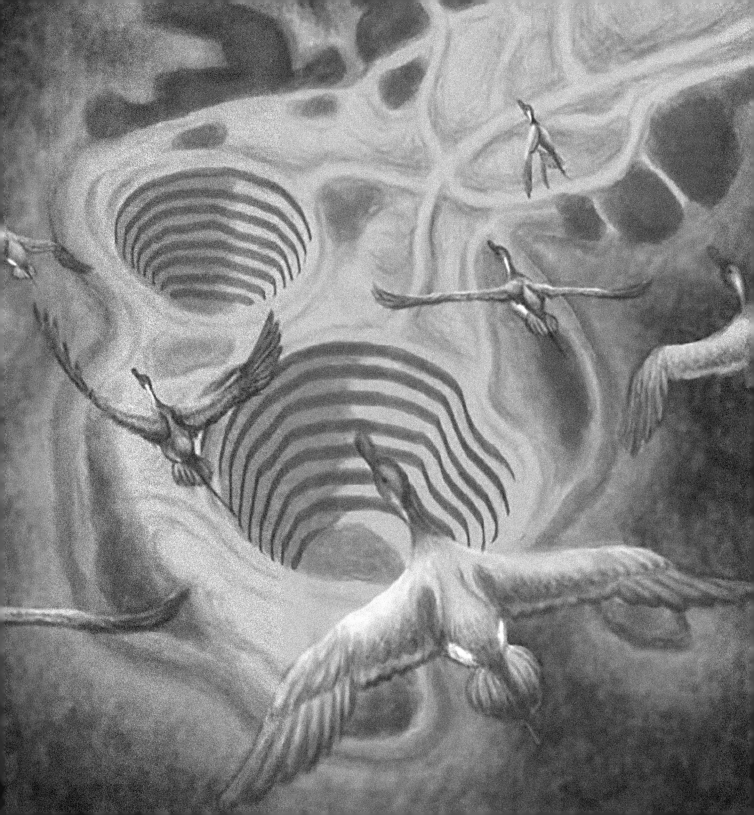

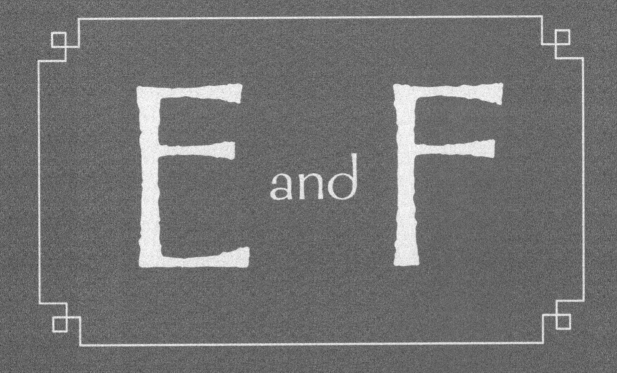

E and F

EAGLES AND ERMINE
SHARE THE EARTH AND
SKY WITH FAWNS, FISHERS,
AND FLEABANE DAISIES.

AN ARCTIC GRAYLING
GLISTENS AS IT
GLIDES THROUGH
GREAT SLAVE LAKE.

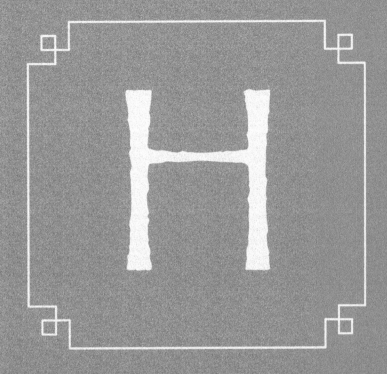

HARNESSED HUSKIES
HAUL HUMANS
NEAR HOOTALINQUA.

ISAAC WEARS IGAAK
WHEN HE BUILDS
HIS IGLOO.

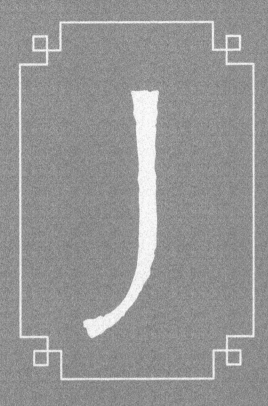

JUNCOS JUMP FROM
JACKPINE TO JUNIPER.

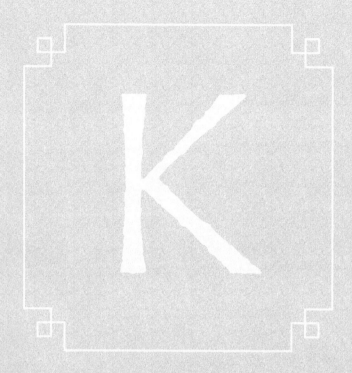

KRINGAYARK KAYAKS
NEAR KETCHIKAN.

L

LADYBUGS LINGER ON
LOUSEWORT LEAVES.

A MUSKRAT MEANDERS
THROUGH THE MUSKEG.

NARWHALS ADMIRE
THE NORTHERN LIGHTS
IN NUNAVUT.

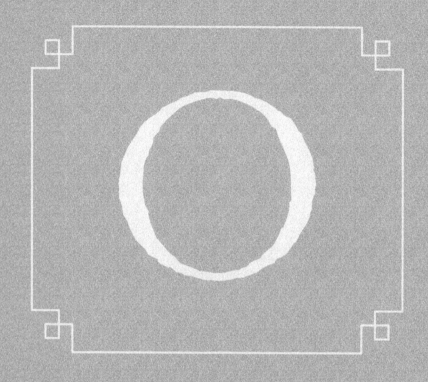

OODLES OF OOKPIKS
OCCUPY OUR TOYBOX.

PAULOOSIE'S PURPLE
PARKA IS PATTERNED
WITH POLAR BEARS
AND PTARMIGAN.

QIVIUT IS QUITE A BIT
COZIER THAN CASHMERE.

RAVENS ARE ROGUES WHO
ROUTINELY RUMMAGE
THROUGH RUBBISH.

SAAKU SMILES AS
HE SMOOTHS AND
SHAPES SOAPSTONE.

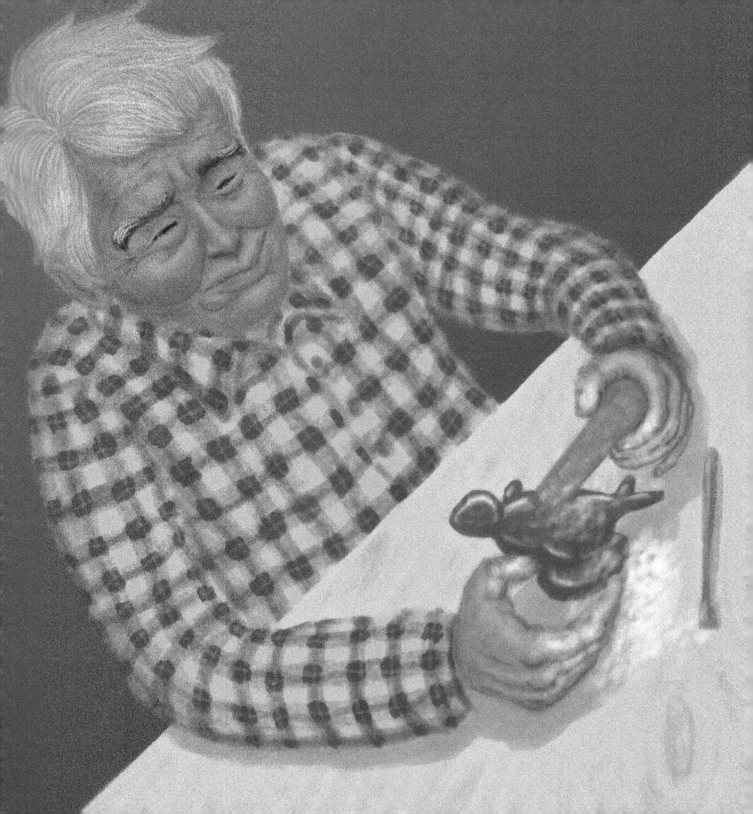

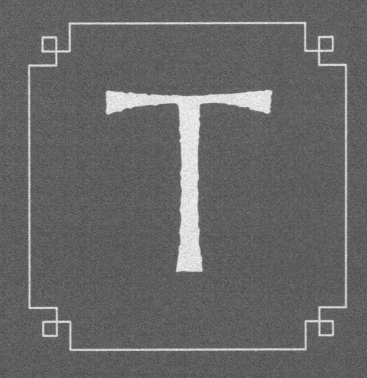

THOMAS TRUDGES
ACROSS THE TUNDRA
TOWARD HIS TUPIQ.

UNA'S ULU IS A VERY
USEFUL UTENSIL.

A VIXEN WATCHES HER
KITS AS VOLES PLAY
AMONG THE VETCH.

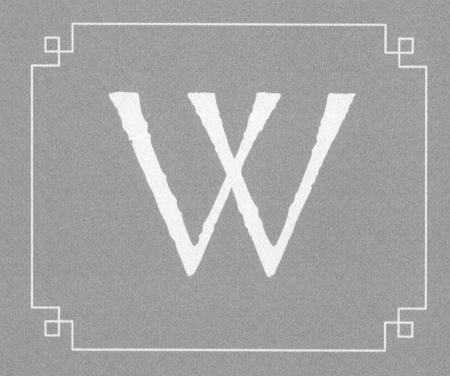

A WALRUS'S WHISKERS
WHITEN AS IT WAITS.

X and Y

XANTHORIA LICHEN AND
YARROW BOTH GROW
NEAR YELLOWKNIFE.

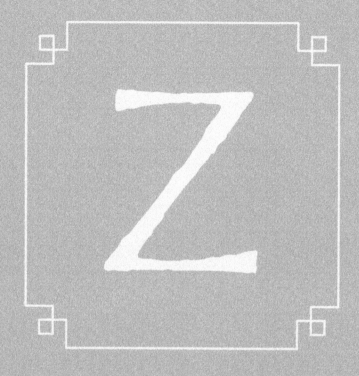

Z

A ZAMBONI ZOOMS
AROUND THE ARCTIC
WINTER GAMES
COMPLEX IN IQALUIT.

A Glossary of Interesting Words

A — AKLAVIK

Aklavik is a hamlet in Canada's Northwest Territories.

B — BELUGAS

Belugas are the smallest of all whales. Their skin is white, and they live in Arctic and sub-Arctic waters.

C — CLOUDBERRIES

Cloudberries are an herb native to alpine, Arctic tundra and boreal forests. They produce amber coloured edible fruit similar to a raspberry.

D — DIAMOND MINE

The first commercial production of diamonds in Canada was in 1998. By 2006, three major mines were producing over 13 million carats per year. Canada is the world's third largest producer of gem quality diamonds.

E — ERMINE

Ermine are small carnivores of the weasel family. In summer, their coats are dark brown above and creamy white below with a black tip on their tails. In winter their coats turn white except for the tip of their tails, which remains black.

F — FLEABANE DAISY

Fleabane daisies are wild, edible and nutritious plants that produce daisy-like blooms. They grow easily in poor soil conditions.

G — GRAYLING

Arctic grayling are a species of freshwater fish in the salmon family. They are abundant throughout Canada's north and a favourite of sport fishers.

H — HOOTALINQUA

Taken from the Northern Tutchone word *hudinlin,* Hootalinqua means "running against the mountain." Historically, many First Nations gathered here to hunt, fish, trade, and socialize. They travelled on the river in the summertime and by foot and dog team in the winter.

I — IGAAK

Igaak are wooden sunglasses that the Inuit people invented to prevent snow blindness. Snow blindness is a dangerous and very painful condition that is caused by the reflection of the sun off the snow.

J — JUNCOS

Juncos are members of the American sparrow family, they live all over North America and far into the Arctic. They like to hop around on the ground.

K — KAYAK

The kayak is a one-person boat created by the Inuit. Originally, they were made from wooden frames covered in sealskin. They were primarily used for hunting.

L — LADYBUG

The ladybug is one of Canada's most beloved insects. They are born black and develop their beautiful bright colouring and spots in the first few weeks of life. Many people believe that ladybugs are good luck charms.

M – MUSKRAT

The muskrat is a large rodent who makes its home in marshes, swamps and wetlands. The muskrat lives all over North America. Historically, they were trapped for their fur.

N – NARWHAL

The narwhal is the unicorn of the sea; it is a pale coloured porpoise that lives in Arctic waters. The males have spiral tusks that can grow up to eight metres long.

O – OOKPIK

An *ookpik* is a popular Inuit handcrafted toy. It is a small owl with a large head and big eyes. They are often made of wolf fur or sealskin. Ookpik is the Inuit word for snowy owl.

P – PTARMIGAN

Ptarmigan are a small group of birds in the grouse family. They have feathered feet and toes as an adaptation to living in the Arctic.

Q – QIVIUT

Qiviut is the soft under wool of the muskox and is naturally shed each spring. Qiviut is stronger and warmer than sheep's wool and softer than cashmere.

R – RAVEN

The common raven, also known as the northern raven, is a large all black bird. Ravens can live up to 21 years in the wild and are successful because of their intelligence.

T – TUPIQ

A *tupiq* is a traditional Inuit tent made from seal or caribou skin.

U – ULU

An *ulu* (or woman's knife) is a curved all-purpose knife used by the Inuit people. It has many uses and can be used to skin and clean animals, cut hair, prepare food, or trim blocks of snow and ice when building an igloo.

V – VIXEN

A vixen is a female fox.

W – WALRUS

The walrus is a large-flippered marine mammal that lives in Arctic waters. They have mustaches and long tusks and lay on the ice near breathing holes hoping to catch their dinner.

X – XANTHORIA ELEGANS

Xanthoria elegans is commonly known as the elegant sunburst lichen. It is bright orange in colour and grows on rocks near bird or rodent perches.

Y – YARROW

Yarrow is an herb that grows between 30 and 70 cm tall. It has strong smelling flowers that look like lace. It spreads quickly and grows in dry rocky places

Z – ZAMBONI

A zamboni is a machine that cleans and resurfaces ice on skating rinks. It was invented in 1949 by Frank Zamboni.

Did You Know? There are some 60 distinct languages among Indigenous First Nations, Dene, Inuit, and Métis in Canada. They group into 12 distinct cultures.

Source: Statistics Canada, 2011 Census

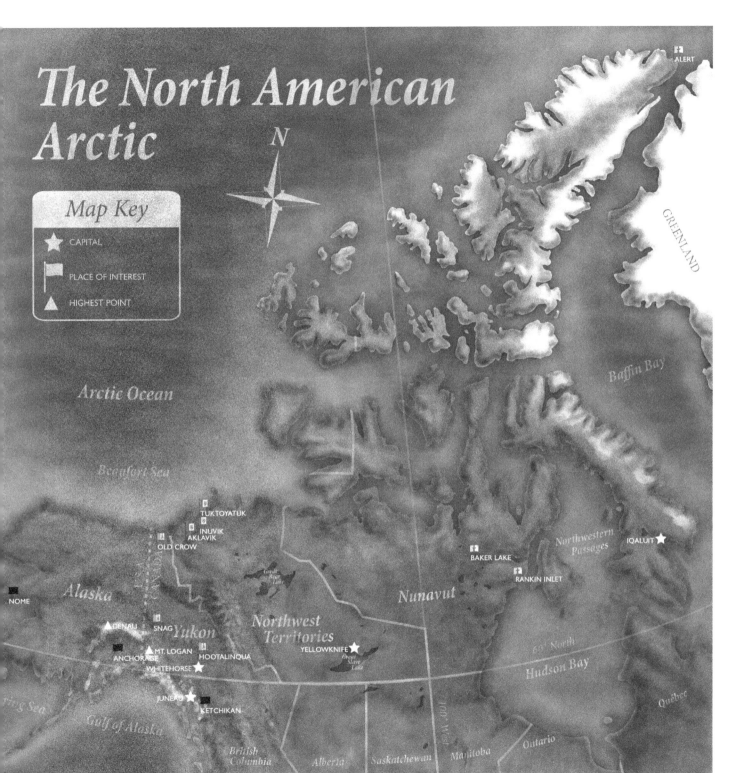

Interesting Facts About the North

ABOUT ALASKA

- Alaska has more coastline than the rest of the United States combined (more than 34,000 miles).

- The highest point in North America is Denali, formerly called Mt. McKinley. The summit elevation is 20,310 feet above sea level.

- There are more than 3,000 rivers and three million lakes in Alaska.

ABOUT YUKON

- The coldest temperature ever recorded in Canada was -63°C, on February 3, 1957 in Snag, Yukon.

- Tools dating back 20,000 years are the first evidence of history in Canada. They were found in caves on the banks of the Bluefish River in northern Yukon. The caves are southwest of the Vuntut Gwichin First Nation.

- Mt. Logan is the highest mountain in Canada, the summit is just under 20,000 feet.

ABOUT THE NORTHWEST TERRITORIES

- Two of the largest lakes in the world are found in the Northwest Territories: Great Bear Lake and Great Slave Lake.

- Tuktoyaktuk is an Inuvialuit hamlet located north of the Arctic Circle on the shore of the Arctic Ocean. It is connected to the rest of Canada by the Inuvik-Tuktoyaktuk Highway, which was officially opened on November 15, 2017.

- The Northern Lights are visible nearly 250 days of the year in the Northwest Territories, more than anywhere else in the world.

ABOUT NUNAVUT

- The territory of Nunavut takes up ⅕th of Canada's total land area: 2.093 million km².

- Half of the world's population of endangered polar bears live in Nunavut.

- The village of Alert, in Nunavut, is the northernmost permanent settlement in the world. It is situated on the northeastern tip of Ellesmere Island.

Acknowledgements

I would like to acknowledge all the peoples of the four northern territories of North America, whose way of life, art, and culture have fascinated me for years and inspired me to write this book.

I hope readers who are unfamiliar with the North will gain some knowledge and appreciation of the beauty and vastness of the land and the tenacity and ingenuity of the people.

To the many different linguistic and cultural groups in the Arctic, thank you for your faithful stewardship of the land and resources over many centuries. Your contributions to our countries, have been, and will continue to be, important and invaluable. I offer you my sincere thank you, *merci beaucoup, mahsi cho, quanani, koana, miigwetch.*

FriesenPress

Suite 300 - 990 Fort St
Victoria, BC, V8V 3K2
Canada

www.friesenpress.com

Illustrated by Morgan Wellborn

ISBN
978-1-5255-2592-6 (Hardcover)
978-1-5255-2593-3 (Paperback)
978-1-5255-2594-0 (eBook)

1. JUVENILE NONFICTION, READERS, BEGINNER

Distributed to the trade by The Ingram Book Company

CPSIA information can be obtained
at www.ICGtesting.com
Printed in the USA
LVHW07s0736290918
591773LV00009B/18/P

9 781525 525933